WHAT'S THE STORY?

Games and activities for creative storymaking

Steve Bowkett

A & C BLACK

Contents

About this book   4

Characters

Making up characters   5
    Heads or tails?   6
    Character questions   7
    Roll a character   8
    Character gallery   9

Profiles   10
    Take a look   11
    On the inside   12
    Memorable moments   13

Character types   14
    Science-fiction characters   15
    Character grid   16
    Super grid   17

Character thumbnails   18
    Thumbnail gallery   19
    Mystery characters   20

Settings

Choosing a setting   21
    Where am I?   22
    Setting grid   23

Setting thumbnails   24
    One cold windy night...   25
    Thumbnail puzzles   26

Plots

Sequencing   27
    Picture mix-up   28
    Make up a plot   29

Story paths   30
    Space Cops   31
    Dinosaur adventure   32
    Make a story path   33

Story maps — 34
  Map it out: 1 — 35
  Map it out: 2 — 36

Smart stars — 37
  Story questions — 38
  Brainstorming ideas — 39

Story motifs — 40
  Speak up! — 41
  What's the genre? — 42
  Genre scenes — 43
  Motif match — 44

Story trees — 45
  Mystery hotel — 46
  The magic box — 47

Contexts — 48
  Questions, questions! — 49
  Spidergram — 50
  The secret of the door — 51

Story masks — 52
  What's going on? — 53
  Picture it — 54
  A narrow escape — 55

Atmospheres

Exploring pictures — 56
  The rope swing — 57
  The dragon flies by — 58
  A journey in the dark — 59
  The hut in the woods — 60

Drafting

Story notebooks — 61
  Sample notebook — 62
  Using a notebook — 63

Suggestions for further reading — 64

About this book

Whether you're a professional writer or a beginner, you are likely to have the same questions when you start a new story: How do I begin? Who are the main characters? How will the story develop?

What's the Story? will help children get the ball rolling. It's packed with games and activities to spark their imaginations, develop creative thinking skills, help them to feel safe and confident in their storymaking and establish a sound platform for the development of literacy skills.

All the activities support the text-level objectives in the National Literacy Strategy *Framework for Teaching* for Years 3 to 6. (Specific references to the National Literacy Strategy text-level units are at the beginning of each chapter.)

The book is divided into five parts, each dealing with a different, key element of storymaking: characters, settings, plots, atmospheres and drafting, and within each part there is a variety of photocopiable activity sheets. These are designed to help children generate and organise ideas during the early stages of storymaking.

The activities in each chapter become progressively more challenging, but it's not necessary to work through the book in order – you can start anywhere, selecting a range of activities to suit the needs and abilities of the children. The teachers' pages suggest how to get started, ways of using the games for extended storymaking and how to link the activities. Most of the worksheets can be adapted to make them easier or more difficult, or to focus on a different genre, simply by masking and substituting parts of the text.

The games and activities in *What's the Story?* have all been developed and tested in schools.

As a writer myself, my attitude to creative writing incorporates curiosity, a sense of fun and willingness to experiment, along with an understanding that nothing is perfect and I can always learn to do things better. I hope that the games in this book will help children to develop this attitude themselves.

Steve Bowkett

Making up characters

Believable characters are essential ingredients when you are storymaking. A writer needs to invent well-rounded characters (in terms of both appearance and personality) to help the reader build up a physical picture of them _and_ understand and predict their behaviour in different situations.

The games

The following games allow the children to build up detailed character profiles without feeling they might get the 'wrong' answer. In **Heads or tails?** and **Character questions**, the children toss a coin to determine characteristics, including physical appearance, background and personality. **Roll a character** and **Character gallery** focus on personality. In these two games, the children use a dice instead of a coin, which gives answers on a sliding scale of one to six.

NLS: Y3 T1 2,10 • Y3 T2 3,8 • Y4 T1 1,2,11 • Y4 T2 2 • Y5 T1 3,15 • Y5 T3 9

Tips

Emphasise to the children that they can't get a 'wrong' answer, but that well thought-out questions lead to more useful answers. The children should ask simple questions such as, 'Does my character like animals?', rather than multi-faceted ones such as, 'Is my character a tall boy with fair hair and blue eyes?'

More ideas

In small groups, the children could make up stories involving their characters. Provide a starting event or situation, for example, the characters find a golden statue buried in a garden or are stranded on a rocky island. Alternatively, you could use a familiar setting, such as at school or at home. Ask the children what their characters would do. During the telling of the story, the children could develop the characters, for example, one who seems mean might turn out to be generous, or may become even meaner.

Linked activities

Coins and dice can be used in similar ways for choosing settings and character types, and for making up plots. See the chapters **Character types**, **Choosing a setting**, **Story maps** and **Story trees**.

Heads or tails?

- Toss a coin to choose Heads or Tails for each pair.
- Circle the word.

	Heads	Tails
character	boy adult	girl child
hair	long fair straight	short dark curly
eyes	blue small	brown large
nose	pointed	rounded
mouth	wide	narrow
personality	friendly shy lazy nervous	unfriendly confident hard-working calm
body	tall slim	short plump
shoulders	broad	narrow
skin	pale	dark
appearance	scruffy	smart

- Now draw your character on the poster.
- Make up a name and describe him or her.

Wanted !

Name: _____

_____

Description: _____

_____

_____

_____

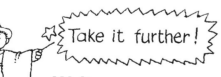

☆ Take it further!

- **Write some more pairs of adjectives.**
- **Toss a coin to choose one word from each pair.**
- **Describe your character to a friend.**

Teachers' note The activity can be used to build up a profile of a specific type of character, such as an extra-terrestrial creature or a historical character. Ask the children to think up appropriate pairs of adjectives. They can go on to write things the characters might say.

What's the Story?
© A & C Black 2001

Character questions

Read the questions.

- **Answer them by tossing a coin.**

Heads = yes
Tails = no

Questions   **Answers**

1. Are you female?   —————

2. Are you an adult?   —————

3. Do you have long hair?   —————

4. Are you tall?   —————

5. Do you dress smartly?   —————

6. Are you very clever?   —————

7. Do you have lots of friends? —————

8. Are you moody?   —————

9. ———————————————— —————

10. ——————————————— —————

11. ——————————————— —————

12. ——————————————— —————

13. ——————————————— —————

14. ——————————————— —————

15. ——————————————— —————

- **Write some more yes/no questions in the spaces.**

- **Toss a coin to find the answers.**

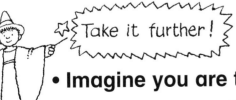
Take it further!

- **Imagine you are the character. How would you describe yourself?**

- **Write a short letter introducing yourself to a penfriend.**

Teachers' note As a further extension, ask the children to play the part of the character they have created and talk to a partner as though they are meeting for the first time. If possible, arrange for the children to write real letters or emails to penfriends at another school.

What's the Story?
© A & C Black 2001

Roll a character

- **Work with a friend.**
- **Complete the list of questions you want to ask your character.**
- **Take turns to ask a question and roll a dice.**
  Look at the key to find out what each number means.
- **Fill in the answers.**

Questions	Answers

Key 🎲
1 = not at all
2 = a little bit
3 = averagely
4 = rather
5 = very
6 = extremely

1. How clever are you? _____

2. How happy are you? _____

3. How popular are you? _____

4. How moody are you? _____

5. How bad is your worst temper? _____

6. How ambitious are you? _____

7. How shy are you? _____

8. How generous are you? _____

9. How attractive are you? _____

10. _____ _____

11. _____ _____

12. _____ _____

13. _____ _____

14. _____ _____

15. _____ _____

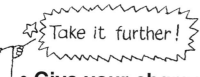
☆ ⭐Take it further!

- **Give your character a name.**
- **Choose a scene from a book you have read.**
- **Imagine your character is there. What would he or she do?**
- **Write what happens.**

Teachers' note The children could be given lists of adjectives to help them make up the extra questions. The game could be linked with word-level work on synonyms and antonyms.

What's the Story?
© A & C Black 2001

Character gallery

- **Choose two characters. Make up their names.**
- **Think of ten questions to ask them.**
- **Roll a dice to find the answers.**

Questions	Answers
	Name: ___ Name: ___

1. How brave are you? _____ _____

2. _____ _____ _____

3. _____ _____ _____

4. _____ _____ _____

5. _____ _____ _____

6. _____ _____ _____

7. _____ _____ _____

8. _____ _____ _____

9. _____ _____ _____

10. _____ _____ _____

- **Write a sentence to describe each character.**

Take it further!

- **Choose one of these situations.**
- **Imagine your characters are there.**
- **Make up a conversation between them.**

A train journey

Lost in a wood

A robbery

Teachers' note Encourage the children to build up in-depth character profiles, for example, ask them questions which begin, 'What would your character do if...?' This will make it easier for the children to predict a character's behaviour in a given situation and to write convincing dialogue.

What's the Story?
© A & C Black 2001

Profiles

Giving characters moods, emotions and a 'past' helps a writer to shape the characters and predict how they might react in certain situations. It is much easier to come up with storylines when you explore and develop the characters in this way.

The games

These activities help children to create more in-depth character profiles. **Take a look** focuses on the physical appearance of a character and encourages the children to use plenty of detail in their character descriptions. **On the inside** investigates facial expressions and body posture. In **Memorable moments**, the children build a character's past by plotting 'real-life' experiences on a time-line.

NLS: Y3 T2 8 • Y4 T1 1,2,3,11 • Y5 T1 3

Tips

To introduce facial expressions and emotions, discuss how it feels when you are nervous, happy, expecting something pleasant and so on. The children may find it helpful to use comparisons when describing emotions, for example, 'My feeling of friendship towards Carl is soft and cosy like a cat curled up in front of the fire.' They could also mime or role-play facial expressions and body postures. Discuss major 'life events' with the children, such as starting and leaving school, becoming independent or getting a job, as well as regular events such as birthdays and anniversaries.

More ideas

The children could act the parts of their characters and use role-play to find out about the personalities and pasts of other characters. Choose a situation, such as waiting at an airport. Ask the children to imagine the world through the eyes of their character and have a conversation with a partner. This can then be developed as a story written in dialogue.

Linked activities

These techniques for building character profiles can help the children to integrate their characters successfully into a plot, for example in the **Story maps** and **Story trees** games.

Take a look

- **Write in the boxes to show what this character looks like.**
- **Draw extra details on the picture.**

You could ask questions and toss a coin to decide the answer.

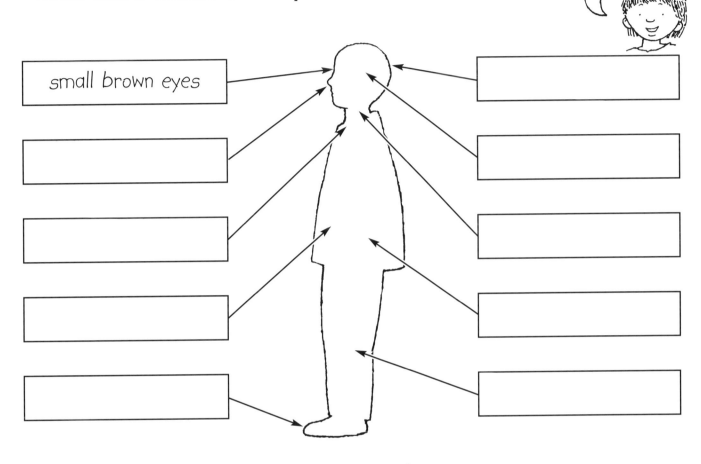

small brown eyes

- **Write phrases to answer these questions.**

How does your character dress? _____

How does he or she walk? _____

How does he or she talk? _____

Take it further!

- **Imagine your character has stolen something. You are a witness.**
- **Write a witness statement describing the character.**

I was walking along Victoria Avenue when I spotted...

Teachers' note Provide thesauruses and dictionaries, and encourage children to use interesting adjectives, for example, instead of 'thin', they could use 'slender' or 'skinny', depending on the effect they want to create. Word banks and photographs of people from clothing catalogues are useful resources for this activity.

What's the Story?
© A & C Black 2001

On the inside

The expression on your face, and the way you stand and move, show how you are feeling.

- **Look at these characters.**
- **Write how you think they are feeling.**

_____

_____

_____

_____

_____

_____

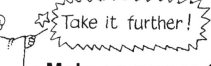

- **Make up names for the characters.**
- **Think of a plot that links some of them together.**
- **Write a short outline of the plot.**

Teacher's note Collect similes, metaphors and phrases and sayings related to emotions, for example, 'She was green with envy.' Encourage the children to make up their own figures of speech. They could draw pictures of situations and then explore possible words to use.

What's the Story?
© A & C Black 2001

Memorable moments

- **Choose a character.**
- **Think of important things that have happened or might happen in his or her life. Write and draw them on the time-line.**

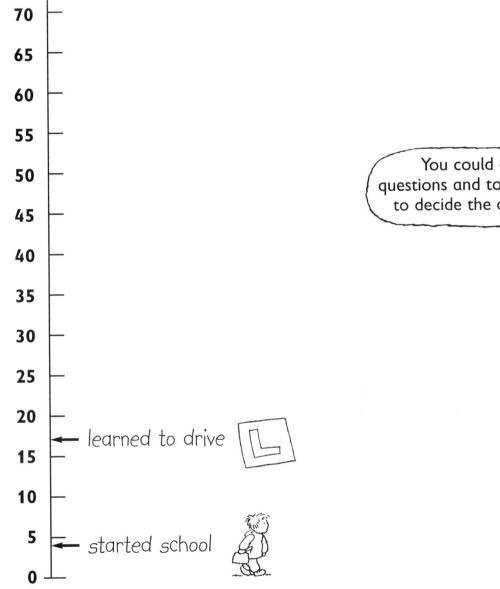

learned to drive

started school

You could ask questions and toss a coin to decide the answer.

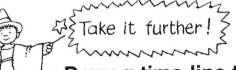

Take it further!

- **Draw a time-line to show 12 months, from January to December.**
- **Write and draw events that could happen to your character in 12 months.**

Teachers' note The children should use a character that they have created in a previous activity. You could draw more time-lines covering different time periods, such as one month, five years or ten years, and ask the children to complete them for the same character.

What's the Story?
© A & C Black 2001

Stock character

A stock character is the kind of character you would expect to find in a particular genre, for example, a villain in a fairy tale. A writer can use stock characters as starting points; adding distinctive or unusual features will prevent them becoming stereotypes.

The games

These games are all based around character grids. Grids are an extremely useful means of helping children to think systematically about character types, and how they compare. Grids can be used to help children analyse characters in texts they have read and to create a variety of new characters for a story. Before starting to fill one in, discuss the character type that will occupy each box. **Science-fiction characters** looks at the genre of science fiction, but you can use a character grid to consider character types in any genre, using parameters such as brave/cowardly; foolish/wise; kind/unkind; intelligent/unintelligent and so on. The **Character grid** is provided for this purpose. Once the children are familiar with the grid format, use the **Super grid** to combine ideas.

NLS: Y3 T2 3 • Y4 T1 2 • Y4 T2 1 • Y5 T1 3 • Y6 T2 10

Tips

As an introduction to character types, ask the children to list some of the choices they have made since the beginning of the day, including ways in which they interacted with other children. Discuss the different ways in which people respond to the same situation. Then encourage them to think about how different characters might respond to the same choices.

More ideas

The **Character grid** template can be used to explore other aspects of storymaking, such as settings and atmosphere (for ideas see page 21), or for non-fiction topic work: for example, animals could be categorised using the parameters predator/prey; water-based/land-based. The **Character grid** is also useful for randomly selecting a character type to include in a story. Roll a dice once to pick a number (1–6) on the vertical axis, then roll again to pick a number on the horizontal axis. This gives a particular box on the grid and provides a starting point for a new character.

Linked activities

Grids are suitable for use with **Story trees**, where a variety of characters and settings are needed for the different branches on the tree. A grid can help the children to generate ideas.

Science-fiction characters

- **These are science-fiction characters. Their positions on the grid show how good or evil they are and how human or non-human.**
- **Choose three more science-fiction characters. Write them where you think they belong.**
- **Now make up three characters of your own. Write them where you think they belong.**

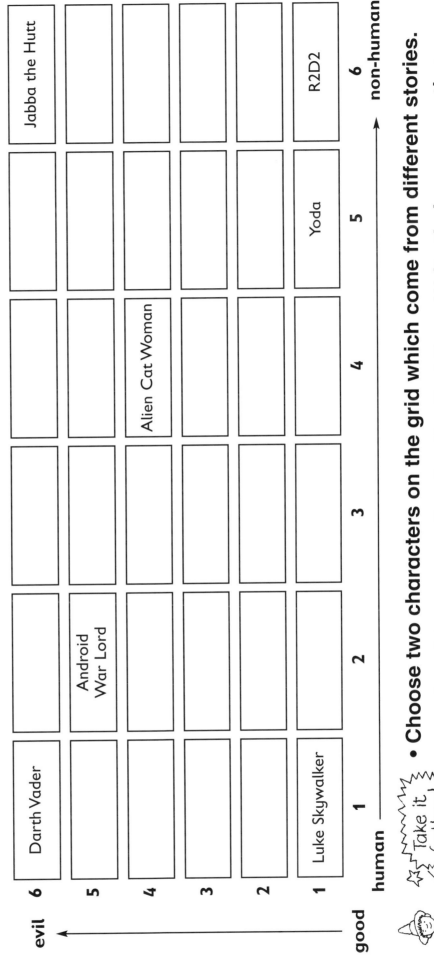

Take it further!
- **Choose two characters on the grid which come from different stories.**
- **Imagine they are meeting for the first time. Write their conversation.**

Teachers' note The characters in this grid all come from Star Wars, with the exception of Alien Cat Woman and Android War Lord, which are made up.

What's the Story?
© A & C Black 2001

15

Character grid

	1	2	3	4	5	6
6						
5						
4						
3						
2						
1						

Teachers' note Write character parameters on the grid before photocopying (for example, young/old; foolish/wise; nervous/calm and so on). You could also fill in some of the boxes with examples taken from shared texts.

What's the Story?
© A & C Black 2001

Super grid

● **Choose characters from other grids you have used. Write them on this Super grid.**

evil ←――――――――――――――――――→ good

weak ←――――――――――――――――――→ powerful

human ←――――――――――――――――――→ non-human

small ←――――――――――――――――――→ large

Teachers' note Examples of characters which could be placed on this grid include a hobbit (bottom left), Harry Potter's friend Hagrid (bottom right) and Harry Potter's enemy Lord Voldemort (top right). Note that the horizontal lines work independently of each other.

What's the Story?
© A & C Black 2001

17

Character thumbnails

A character thumbnail is a brief written description, or even just a heading, often accompanied by a sketch of the character. It gives the bare facts about a person and is a useful starting point for more detailed writing.

The games

These activities encourage children to select the most important information about a character and to express it briefly. **Thumbnail gallery** offers practice in writing simple character descriptions which stick to the main points of interest. **Mystery characters** gives children an opportunity to make up dialogue based on the information in a thumbnail. Encourage them to pick a topic for the dialogue that is relevant to their character, and to use it to find out more about things mentioned in the thumbnail.

NLS: Y3 T1 10 • Y4 T1 11 • Y5 T1 3,15 • Y6 T1 11,14

Tips

To introduce the activities, read with the children entries in a biographical dictionary featuring famous people such as scientists, artists, musicians or historical figures. Encourage the children to notice what kind of information was selected for these brief write-ups. You could then ask them to write a character thumbnail of themselves.

More ideas

The children could research the life of someone they know or a famous person, and decide on the important information to include in a biography (for example, notable achievements, actions and talents). They could write a 'thumbnail' entry for a class or school biographical dictionary. Discuss which tense would be used.

Linked activities

Character thumbnails can be combined with **Setting thumbnails** to provide ideas for starting a story.

Thumbnail gallery

A character thumbnail is a short description which tells you the most interesting things about a character.

- **Read these character thumbnails.**
- **Fill in the missing information.**

The first one has been done for you.

Name: Philippa Stephens

Age: 11

Description: Tall, dark hair, blue eyes, gentle face. She is usually friendly and in a good mood, but can have a terrible temper if things don't go her way. She has one brother, Dave (12), and a cat called Mog (she loves him to bits).

Name: Paula Samra

Age: _____

Description: Long black hair, brown eyes. Paula left school when she was _____ and now works as a _____ _____ . She is usually very _____ and _____ . Her special claim to fame is _____ _____ !

Name: Jason Marsden

Age: 12

Description: _____ _____ _____ .

Jason comes from a _____ family. His hobbies are _____ , _____ and especially _____ . His favourite _____ is _____ .

Name: Ben Leech

Age: _____

Description: _____ _____ _____ .

Ben has led a life full of _____ . At _____ he went to _____ , where he _____ _____ .

⭐ Take it further!

- **Choose a well-known book character. Write a character thumbnail, but don't write the name!**
- **Give it to a friend. Can they work out who it is?**

Teachers' note For further practice, the children could create character thumbnails of themselves, their friends, famous people and characters from stories.

What's the Story?
© A & C Black 2001

Mystery characters

- ## Who are these people?
- ## Make up character thumbnails for them.

Remember to stick to the main interesting points.

Name: _____

Age: _____

Description: _____

_____

_____

_____

_____

_____

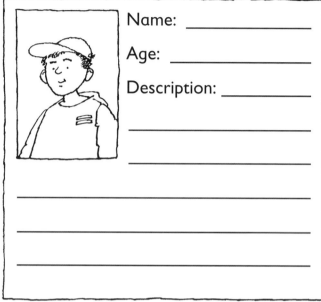

Name: _____

Age: _____

Description: _____

_____

_____

_____

_____

_____

Name: _____

Age: _____

Description: _____

_____

_____

_____

_____

_____

Name: _____

Age: _____

Description: _____

_____

_____

_____

_____

_____

Take it further!

- ## Choose two of the characters.
- ## Write a short conversation between them.

Teachers' note For the extension activity, you could provide the children with the Smart star emotions on page 39. Ask them to choose emotions that the characters might be feeling. The children could also make a time-line for one of the characters (see page 13).

What's the Story?
© A & C Black 2001

Choosing a setting

A vividly described and believable location can make a story really memorable. It leaves the reader with the feeling of having been there. Writers think about settings in relation to characters and plot. The place should influence, and be influenced by, the people in the story, just as in real life.

The games

Setting grids encourage children to imagine a range of settings and locations, and to choose one that suits the genre and mood of their story. **Where am I?** suggests story settings, each of which creates a different atmosphere. **Setting grid** can be used to help children think up other types of settings, using parameters such as hot/cold; flat/rugged; wet/dry; friendly (benign)/dangerous; busy (populated)/empty. Before the children start to fill in a grid, discuss with them the kind of location that will go in each box.

NLS: Y3 T1 1,11,12 • Y4 T1 1 • Y4 T2 2,3,10

Tips

To introduce the activity, encourage the children to list useful words for describing a setting, concentrating on expressive adjectives and powerful verbs. The children could choose a particular setting and make a word-bank for it. Try using pairs of similar descriptions as a basis for discussing atmosphere, for example:

a) There were tall trees.
b) Tall elms loomed on all sides.

a) I heard footsteps behind me. They stopped when I turned to look.
b) The crunch of gravel, the faint crack of a twig; I turned – a crafty silence.

More ideas

Grid templates can be made to any size, depending on the exercise and the children's abilities. It is usually best to start with small grids and work up to larger ones, and there is no need to fill in the whole grid in one go. The children can keep adding to their grids as ideas come to them. A large-scale grid makes a useful classroom display, allowing plenty of space for written descriptions, drawings and pictures cut out of magazines.

Linked activities

Setting grids can be used to help the children think of ideas for **Setting thumbnails**, or to generate possible settings for **Story trees**.

Where am I?

Here are some different settings for stories. As you read <u>along</u> the grid, they become more and more frightening. As you read <u>up</u> the grid, they move from a city to a place in the countryside.

- **Think of places or situations which fit the gaps.**
- **Write them on the grid.**

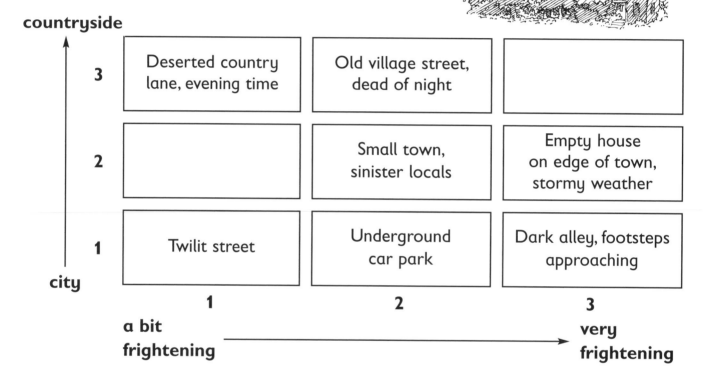

countryside

	1	**2**	**3**
3	Deserted country lane, evening time	Old village street, dead of night	
2		Small town, sinister locals	Empty house on edge of town, stormy weather
1	Twilit street	Underground car park	Dark alley, footsteps approaching

city

a bit frightening → **very frightening**

- **Choose a box and imagine you are there.**
- **Describe how you would feel.**

_____

_____

_____

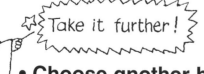

{Take it further!}

- **Choose another box on the grid.**
- **Think of two characters who might be in this setting.**
- **Write what happens next.**

Teachers' note After filling in a character grid, you could ask the children to place the characters in appropriate settings on this grid, for example, an evil wizard might be placed on a dark, storm-swept mountainside.

What's the Story?
© A & C Black 2001

Setting grid

Teachers' note Choose setting parameters for the children to explore and write them on the grid before photocopying (for ideas see page 21). You could also fill in some of the boxes to get them started.

What's the Story?
© A & C Black 2001

Setting thumbnails

A setting thumbnail is a brief description of sights, sounds and smells, with a sketch of the location. It sets the scene and atmosphere and hints at ways you can take the story forward. I use a setting thumbnail either as a 'story starter' or at an exciting point in the story to make the description more vivid.

The games

These games encourage the children to use their different senses to build up a detailed picture of a setting. **One cold windy night...** familiarises children with the various elements that make up a setting thumbnail. **Thumbnail puzzles** offers practice in writing thumbnails, which will inspire the children to include more detail in their own stories. The thumbnails are written in the second person so that the children can either imagine themselves in the scene, or make up a character and put themselves in his or her shoes.

> **NLS:** Y3 T1 6,11,12 • Y4 T1 9 • Y4 T2 10,13 • Y5 T1 11 • Y5 T3 2

Tips

When writing thumbnails, the children should ask themselves questions such as, 'What can I see nearby and in the distance?' 'What can I hear?' 'What can I smell?' Encourage them to 'picture' the scene and to make brief notes rather than full explanations of what is happening. Ask the children to think about what other characters in the scene are doing.

More ideas

Let the children write setting thumbnails of scenes in books they read. This will help them to remember the stories in greater, more vivid detail, while giving them ideas for their own storymaking. The children could also try turning a setting thumbnail into a poem, for example, the first of the **Thumbnail puzzles** might become: Just _____ and _____ / Smiling. / No one else. / A curtain flapped / Waiting / I looked from one to the other. / The curtain flapped. / I spotted the box / On the table... and so on.

Linked activities

Setting thumbnails can be used along with grid work to build up a story setting. See the chapters **Character types** and **Choosing a setting**. Thumbnails can also be incorporated into **Story trees** and **Story paths**.

One cold windy night...

A setting thumbnail is a short description of a scene. It tells you what you can see, hear and smell.

• Read this setting thumbnail.

> It's a cold windy night. It's raining. You can hear the wind booming in the trees and smell the damp earth. You are in the middle of nowhere, having lost your way earlier in the day. Something tells you there is danger not far away. Looking round, you see a light in the distance and wonder if you will find refuge there…

• Underline the words which help you to imagine the scene.

• The description is written in the second person.

Why do you think this is? _____

_____

• Fill in the gaps in this setting thumbnail.

Look at the picture to help you.

> You are at the funfair. It is a pleasant sunny day and the fair is full of people having fun. You can hear _____ and smell _____. Suddenly a piercing scream rings out. Something is wrong. You look round and see _____

☆ Take it further!

• Imagine you are at the funfair.

• What has just happened? What might happen next?

Write a paragraph continuing the story.

Teachers' note For each thumbnail, the children could list suitable words and phrases for describing the sights, sounds and smells. They could then choose the most effective ones and use them as the basis of a story or poem.

What's the Story?
© A & C Black 2001

Thumbnail puzzles

• **Fill in the gaps in these setting thumbnails. Make the scenes as vivid as you can.**

There was no one in the room apart from _____ and _____. This was a very special occasion, when _____ would at last be settled. They were both smiling, and yet you felt strangely nervous. _____ said, '_____? _____!' and then opened the box. What happened next took you completely by surprise. '_____!'

The party was in full swing. All the guests had arrived, except for _____, which made you feel very disappointed. Nearby you could hear _____, while further away _____ echoed over the _____. Without warning _____ whizzed by, startling everyone. You _____ just in time to see _____. _____ screamed, but by then it was too late, because _____.

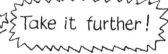

Take it further!

• **Draw three pictures. Draw one showing a place, one showing the weather and one showing an event that is about to happen.**

• **Swap your pictures with a friend. Write a setting thumbnail that matches the pictures.**

Teachers' note This could be linked with sentence level work on powerful verbs and expressive adjectives.

What's the Story?
© A & C Black 2001

Sequencing

Learning to put events in a logical order is an important skill in storymaking. Visual aids can help, and are a good way of developing creative thinking. Although there are many possible routes that a story can take, the final sequence of events should leave the reader thinking, 'Yes, of course it had to happen that way.'

The games

The following games help children to generate storylines by providing them with solid ideas to spark their imaginations. **Picture mix-up** and **Make up a plot** provide a variety of pictures which the children cut out and use in any order to make a story idea. Lots of different plots can be made up by changing the order of the pictures and choosing different ones as the starting point.

NLS: Y3 T2 7 • Y3 T3 1,10 • Y4 T1 3,4,15 • Y6 T2 1

Tips

For further games of this kind you could use clip art, which is readily available on CD-ROM and via the Internet, much of it copyright free. It can be readily imported into a word-processing package such as Microsoft Word, enabling children to create an illustrated story and also practise their IT skills. Using web-page building software, the children could build animated visual files (GIF files) and sound files (WAV files) into a story. The technology does take some mastering, but the results are very satisfying. The reader scrolls through or mouse-clicks on designated spots, and the written text comes to life with animations and sounds.

More ideas

Instead of writing a narrative in chronological order, the children could use the pictures as 'triggers' for flashbacks in a story. Alternatively, they could sort the pictures into two sets and tell two separate storylines which eventually come together and intertwine.

Linked activities

Sequencing can be used to explore different genres, along with the activities in **Story motifs**. The pictures can also be used as inspiration for **Story paths**, **Story maps** and **Story trees**.

Picture mix-up

- Cut out the pictures.
- Use them to help you make up a story plot. You can use as many pictures as you like, in any order.
- Glue the pictures in order on a piece of paper. Write your story plot beneath.

☆ Take it further!

- Look at the pictures in reverse order, starting with the last picture.
- Think of a new story plot that uses the pictures in this order. Write it on a new piece of paper.

Teachers' note The children could tell a mystery story as a series of scenes, experienced by a narrator. In each brief scene the children need to introduce a hint of mystery, for example, seagulls suddenly rise squawking from a field or beach.

What's the Story?
© A & C Black 2001

Make up a plot

- **Cut out the pictures.**
- **Use them to help you write a story plot.**

Include as many pictures as you can.

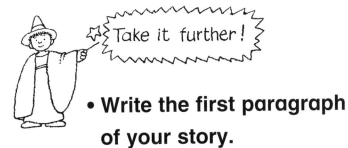

☆ Take it further!

- **Write the first paragraph of your story.**

Think about the characters and the setting.

Teachers' note You or the children could first decide on the genre of story to be written, for example, a mystery, an adventure, a tale with a moral, a science-fiction story, a humorous story or a story about an issue such as bullying, taking responsibility, or pollution.

What's the Story?
© A & C Black 2001

Story paths

Before starting to write a story, it is useful to know where the plot is going and how the final outcome will be reached. Organising the plot and recording it in a logical and ordered way helps a writer to think through the path of events.

The games

The activities in this chapter allow children to plan a story in a simple linear way. The activities develop children's skills in sequencing events and help them to see that a story has a definite structure which breaks down – often easily and naturally – into a number of scenes, or 'chunks'. Creating story paths is a simple and enjoyable way of plotting a story as well as being a useful exercise before beginning a first draft.

> **NLS:** Y3 T2 6,7 • Y3 T3 1,10 • Y4 T1 3,4 • Y5 T1 14 • Y6 T2 1

Tips

Story path templates can be any size and feature any number of boxes, but it is important that the children have plenty of space for writing. If possible, enlarge **Make a story path** to A3 size. Encourage the children to draw pictures on and around their paths to illustrate their stories. Once the children have finalised the plot, they can return to individual boxes to add further ideas and details.

More ideas

The children could plot any story they have read on a story path. Simple traditional tales work particularly well with this approach, for example, *Puss in Boots*, *The Gingerbread Man*, *Little Red Riding Hood* and *The Wizard of Oz*. A story path can also be used in other areas of the curriculum, for example to tell a historical account or to retell a parable. As an alternative to a story path template, the children could write scenes or 'story chunks' on file cards and put them in sequence. The larger the file cards, the more space there is for the children to return and add descriptive details, new ideas, dialogue and so on.

Linked activities

Character thumbnails and **Setting thumbnails** can be added to a story path to provide extra detail.

Space Cops

A story path shows the main events of a story in order.

The events can be shown in words or in pictures.

- **Follow the story path to read the story so far.**
- **What might happen next? Write and draw in the empty boxes to finish the story.**

Put one event in each box.

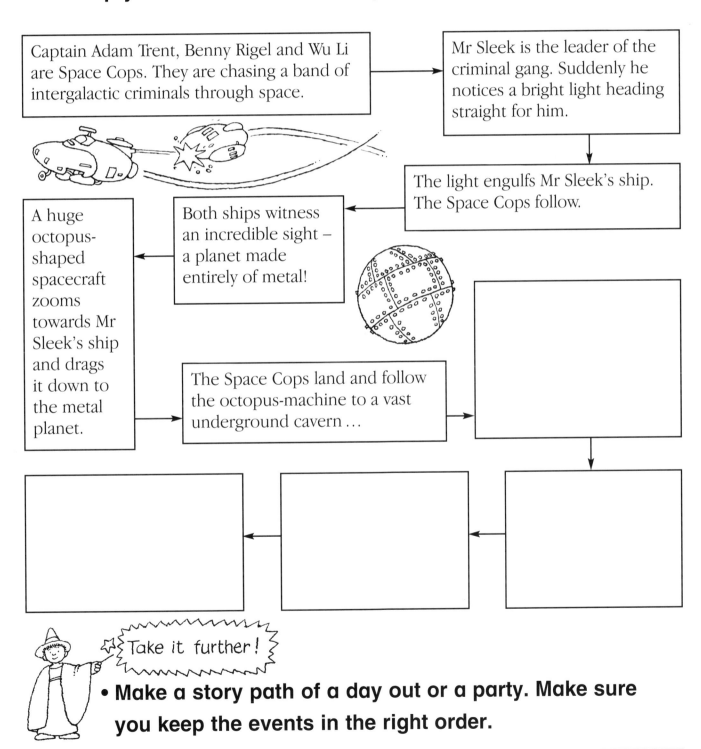

Captain Adam Trent, Benny Rigel and Wu Li are Space Cops. They are chasing a band of intergalactic criminals through space.

Mr Sleek is the leader of the criminal gang. Suddenly he notices a bright light heading straight for him.

The light engulfs Mr Sleek's ship. The Space Cops follow.

Both ships witness an incredible sight – a planet made entirely of metal!

A huge octopus-shaped spacecraft zooms towards Mr Sleek's ship and drags it down to the metal planet.

The Space Cops land and follow the octopus-machine to a vast underground cavern …

☆ Take it further!

- **Make a story path of a day out or a party. Make sure you keep the events in the right order.**

Teachers' note The story is taken from *The Planet Machine* by Steve Bowkett (published by A & C Black in the Comix series). Explore the use of short sentences to create suspense or excitement. Also discuss the effects of punctuation such as dashes, colons and exclamation marks.

What's the Story?
© A & C Black 2001

Dinosaur adventure

- **Fill in the gaps in the story path.**
- **Draw pictures around the path to add more detail.**

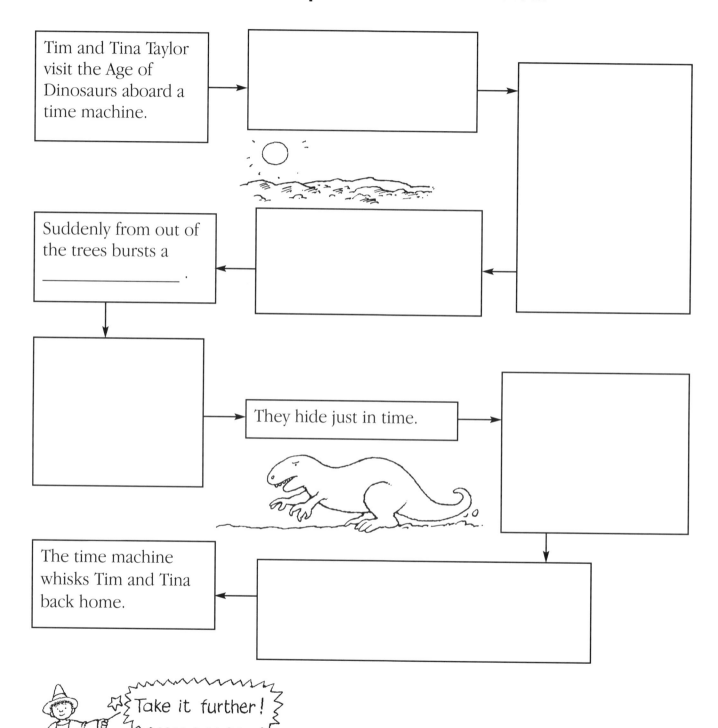

Tim and Tina Taylor visit the Age of Dinosaurs aboard a time machine.

Suddenly from out of the trees bursts a
_____ .

They hide just in time.

The time machine whisks Tim and Tina back home.

Take it further!

- **Choose another time and place that Tim and Tina might visit in the time machine.**
- **Draw a story path for their adventure.**

Teachers' note The children could write about a period they have studied in history, for example, they could imagine that Tim and Tina find themselves inside a pyramid, on board a Viking longship, at the court of Elizabeth of England or in a Victorian school.

What's the Story?
© A & C Black 2001

Make a story path

- **Choose a short story you have read.**
- **Split the story into scenes. Write one or two sentences about each scene.**

> Write each scene in a new box.

Story title: _____

Author: _____

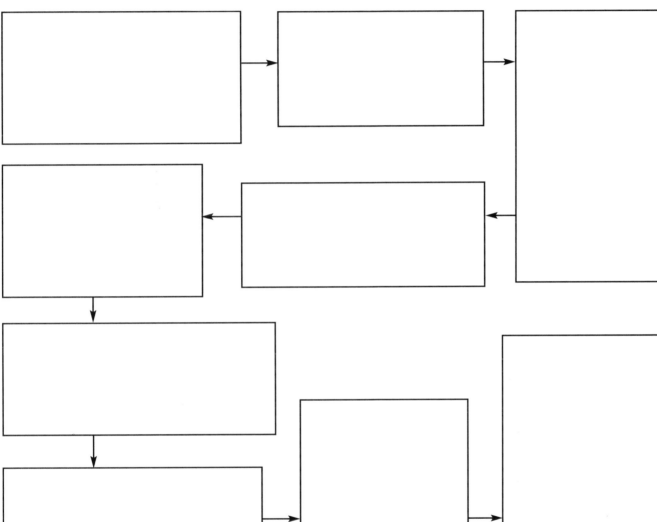

Take it further!

- **Draw another path and plot a new story of your own. You could use one of these ideas to get you started.**

A ship in a storm

A sports competition

A stray dog

Teachers' note Help the children to get started with the extension activity by asking them questions such as, 'What kind of ship is it? What is it carrying?'; 'What sports event is it? What is at stake?'; 'You follow the dog. Where does it take you? What do you discover?'

What's the Story?
© A & C Black 2001

Story maps

A finished story has a linear structure, but a story-in-the-making is more like a map. Story mapping is an exciting way of investigating the setting and the characters before you decide on the final story structure. It works on the notion that having good ideas leads from having _lots_ of ideas!

The game

This game presents the children with a map of a setting which they can fill in by answering questions and adding further details. They then use counters to represent characters and move them around the map to explore the setting. Lots of creative ideas can be developed by weighing up the possible outcomes of each route the characters could take. The children will each need a copy of **Map it out: 1 and 2** and two counters for this game.

NLS: Y3 T2 7 • Y3 T3 13 • Y4 T1 9 • Y4 T2 2 • Y6 T1 7

Tips

At first, story mapping is best done as a teacher-led activity. Ask the children questions about the sights, sounds, smells and textures of the landscape on the map, for example, 'What sounds would the characters hear now?' 'What would that rock in front of them feel like?' You could guide the class through the questions in **Map it out: 2** and map out a storyline together. To prompt further discussion about what might happen next, ask questions such as, 'Are the characters in danger?' 'Why might they decide to split up?' 'Why might they quarrel later in the story?'

More ideas

Once the children are familiar with the exercise, they could work on story maps in small groups. This often leads to fruitful discussion, questioning and negotiation. You could ask different groups of children to explore different areas of the map, each group then reporting back on what they have found. Story maps can be made to show other settings, such as inside a building, in a town, on a strange planet and so on. Similar questions to those in **Map it out: 2** can be asked about the setting and characters.

Linked activities

Story mapping can form a useful introduction to making **Story trees** and to using **Story notebooks**. You can add **Profiles, Character thumbnails** and **Setting thumbnails** to story maps.

Map it out: 1

- **Look at the story map. The crosses indicate two characters.**
- **Make up names for the characters and write them on the map.**
- **Answer the questions on Map it out: 2.**
- **Draw the details on the map.**

Teachers' note Use this with page 36. You could use Smart stars to help the children to think of ideas for their story.

What's the Story?
© A & C Black 2001

35

Map it out: 2

- **Answer the questions.**
- **For yes/no questions, toss a coin and tick the box.**
- **For questions with more than two answers, roll a dice and circle the number.**

Heads = yes
Tails = no

Setting

- Is it night-time?   **yes** ☐ **no** ☐
- What season is it?   **1 spring**   **2 summer**   **3 autumn**   **4 winter**
- Have the characters been to this place before?   **yes** ☐ **no** ☐
- The characters can hear a river. In which direction is it?
  1 north   **2 east**   **3 south**   **4 west**
- Are there any roads or paths?   **yes** ☐ **no** ☐
  Where are they?   **1 north**   **2 east**   **3 south**   **4 west**
- What could be in the distance to the west? Make a list of six things and roll a dice.
- Make a list of other things, such as rocks, trees and animals. Toss a coin for each thing to find out if it is there.

Using the story map

- Make up ten questions about the characters. Answer the questions for each character using a dice, a coin or your own ideas.
- Roll a dice to find out how much the characters like each other.
- Roll a dice to find out how much the characters trust each other.
- Answer these questions to find out what happens next. (Use a counter for each character and move them around the map.)
  - Are the characters lost?
  - Are they in danger?
  - Are they looking for something or someone?
  - What are they saying to each other?
  - They see or hear something unexpected – in which direction?
  - Now what do they do?
- Write your story ideas on a piece of paper.

Teachers' note If there are only four answers to choose from, the children should roll a dice until they get a number between one and four, or they could make a spinner by dividing a square of card into four numbered sections and pushing a pencil through the centre.

What's the Story?
© A & C Black 2001

Smart stars

Smart stars are cards bearing questions or single words, which act as prompts when planning a story – or when you get stuck! They can help a writer decide where the plot is going and how the characters might be feeling, by suggesting questions to think about or words to include in the story.

The games

These activities encourage children to incorporate new ideas during planning, and offer practice in brainstorming. Photocopy **Story questions** on to coloured card and cut out the stars. **Brainstorming ideas** can be either copied on to card and the stars cut out, or the entire sheet can be given to the children during storymaking for them to discuss in pairs or groups. Ask children to pick up smart stars as they plan their stories and act on what the star suggests. It may ask them to follow an instruction, answer a question or brainstorm ideas about a particular word.

> **NLS:** Y3 T1 9 • Y3 T2 7 • Y3 T3 5,13 • Y4 T1 9 • Y4 T2 2 • Y5 T1 15

Tips

Establish rules for when the children use smart stars, for example, they could pick up a star every five minutes; after every *n*th roll of the dice; or when they get stuck. You can arrange the stars face down for the children to pick at random, or allow the children to choose from a selection they can see. If the children do not find a particular message helpful to their story, they need not use it.

More ideas

Give the children blank star shapes and ask them to make their own sets of instructions, questions and words for brainstorming. The children could also use smart stars when reviewing stories they have written, with questions such as, 'What atmosphere are you trying to create?' 'Can you add any detail to help create atmosphere?' 'Are there any words you could make more expressive?' 'Are there any loose ends in the story that you need to tie up?' The stars could be picked at random or you could suggest ones which are appropriate to a particular child.

Linked activities

Smart stars are useful when making **Story maps**. They can also be used while children are writing **Story notebooks,** as prompts for extra things to look out for.

Story questions

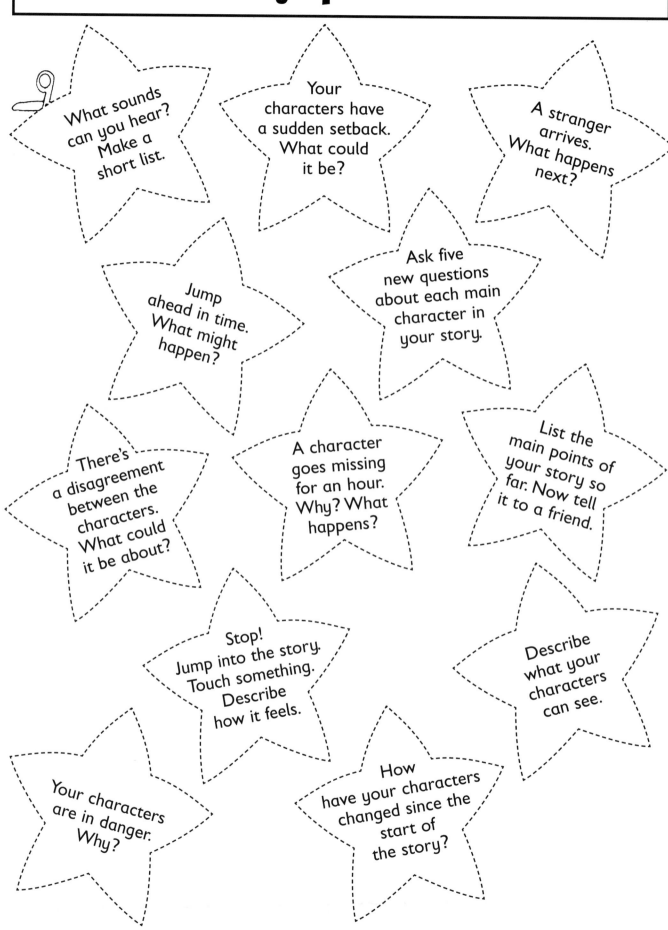

What sounds can you hear? Make a short list.

Your characters have a sudden setback. What could it be?

A stranger arrives. What happens next?

Jump ahead in time. What might happen?

Ask five new questions about each main character in your story.

There's a disagreement between the characters. What could it be about?

A character goes missing for an hour. Why? What happens?

List the main points of your story so far. Now tell it to a friend.

Stop! Jump into the story. Touch something. Describe how it feels.

Describe what your characters can see.

Your characters are in danger. Why?

How have your characters changed since the start of the story?

Teachers' note The messages on the stars could be masked before photocopying. Other messages could be inserted, or they could be left blank for the children to fill in with their own ideas.

What's the Story?
© A & C Black 2001

Brainstorming ideas

Each of these words can have several different meanings.

• **Discuss all the meanings you can think of.**

• **How can you use the words in your story?**

fair turn back lift space drive will trigger step face

It is important to think about how characters in a story are feeling.

• **Discuss why someone might feel these emotions.**

• **Can you use any of them in your story?**

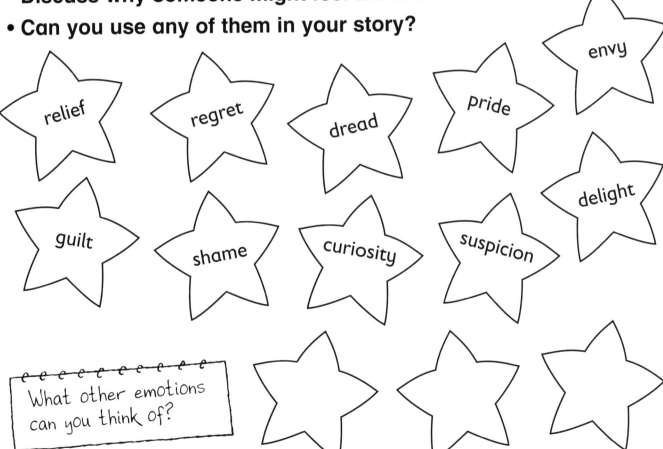

relief regret dread pride envy guilt shame curiosity suspicion delight

What other emotions can you think of?

Teachers' note For the first activity, other words you could use might be: stuck, right, break, way, time, set, look, rest, left, less, leave, take. Examples for the second activity are: anger, disappointment, excitement, fear, hope, impatience, irritation, pity, relief, satisfaction, shock, sorrow, unease.

What's the Story?
© A & C Black 2001

Story motifs

A story motif is a feature or dominant idea which helps the reader recognise the genre of a story. The motif may be a character, a piece of action or dialogue, an expected setting, an object, and so on.

The games

This chapter helps to familiarise children with different genres so that they can identify motifs and use them in their own storymaking. **Speak up!**, **What's the genre?** and **Genre scenes** provide practice in recognising genre and making up story motifs. **Motif match** offers a more challenging set of motifs which the children may interpret in different ways. Motifs provide children with familiar 'hooks', which let them concentrate on other aspects of their writing. The activities can also be used to introduce cliché and stereotype.

> **NLS:** Y3 T1 2 • Y3 T2 2,9 • Y4 T2 8 • Y4 T3 2 • Y5 T2 1,9,11 • Y6 T2 10

Tips

To introduce the games, discuss the idea of genre and ask the children how many different genres they can think of. From the start, emphasise to the children why they are using motifs, and encourage them to do so thoughtfully. Children will often lift ideas from TV and film, but try to guide them to think beyond the obvious.

More ideas

The children could analyse stories they have read and record the motifs on a chart, for example:

Genre: Mystery	
Motif: Characters who are seeking to solve the mystery	
Story Ravensgill by William Mayne	**Characters** Judith, Mick, Bob and Dick

Genre: Fairy tale	
Motif: An evil character	
Story Snow White	**Characters** Wicked stepmother

Linked activities

Genre ties in with many other storymaking activities, including **Story maps**, **Story trees**, **Character thumbnails** and **Setting thumbnails**.

Speak up!

These story characters have lost their voices!

• **What do you think they are saying? Fill in the speech bubbles.**

Adventure

Wait – I think I can hear footsteps! We have to hide!

Mystery

Fantasy

Legend

Fairy tale

Science fiction

Historical fiction

Take it further!

• **Choose three of the story genres.**

• **Write a setting for each one.**

Teachers' note This could be linked with sentence level work on the different ways of demarcating speech. The children could re-write these examples using speechmarks and a verb such as 'said', 'exclaimed', or 'asked'.

What's the Story?
© A & C Black 2001

What's the genre?

- ## Look at these sets of story motifs.
- ## Which genre does each set belong to?

Place	**Person**	**Object**	**Speech**
			'What's that creaking noise?' 'I think it's coming from the cellar!'

Genre

Place	**Person**	**Object**	**Speech**
			'Mighty Odin, give me strength to battle against the dark powers of Abred!'

Genre

Place	**Person**	**Object**	**Speech**
		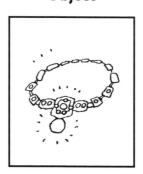	'Look here, these footprints were made by a man with a limp.'

Genre

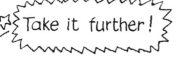

Take it further!

- ## Think of two other story genres.
- ## Write or draw some motifs for each one.

Use a place, a person, an object and a piece of speech.

Teachers' note In groups, the children could create their own motif cards for stories they have read, recording the titles of the stories on the backs of the cards. The cards could be mixed up and passed to another group who sort the cards into story sets and identify the stories.

What's the Story?
© A & C Black 2001

Genre scenes

- **Read this scene from a story.**

> The tall dark wizard strode majestically into the village. He stopped at the young peasant boy's hut and wove a strange sign in the air with his glowing silver staff. 'Show yourself, apprentice,' he called with a slow, sly grin. 'It's time to meet your fate.'

- **Which genre does this belong to?** _____
- **Underline the words which tell you.**

- **Write the genre for this set of story motifs.**
- **Make up a scene like the one at the top of the page.**

> Include a place, a person, an object and a piece of speech.

Place	**Person**	**Object**	**Speech**
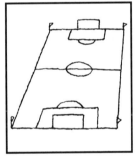			'You can win this if you just believe in yourselves!'

Genre

_____

_____

_____

_____

Take it further!

- **Think of a story you have read. Which genre is it?**
- **Draw some motifs for the story.**

Teachers' note For the extension activity, the children could develop their motif pictures during art lessons. Then they could create a display of the motifs alongside copies of the book to encourage others to read it.

What's the Story?
© A & C Black 2001

Motif match

- Cut out the story motifs and the labels.
- Sort them into genre groups.
- Choose one genre and think of a character.
- Draw a story map.
- Ask ten questions about what happens next.

Adventure	Fantasy	Historical fiction	Romance	Sports stories
			Promises	
The Land Beyond the Horizon				

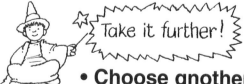

Take it further!

- Choose another group of motifs.
- Think of a story idea and write a plot outline.

Teachers' note You could use the story motifs on this sheet to help the class produce a piece of shared writing. Create a story map on the board or on a flip chart (see page 34).

Story trees

A story-in-the-making offers a range of possibilities for the direction a plot might take. Drawing a story tree lets a writer think through a number of different ideas at the planning stage. He or she can then explore all the ideas and find out where each one will lead.

The games

The following games help the children to think up more interesting and unusual plots and to investigate a variety of storylines. **Mystery hotel** introduces the children to story trees and shows how a variety of ideas can spring from one starting point. **The magic box** encourages the children to make a story tree of their own. They could include thumbnails and motifs to help the plot along and to add detail.

NLS: Y4 T1 9 • Y4 T3 12 • Y5 T1 2,14 • Y6 T2 1 • Y6 T3 14

Tips

Teacher-led group discussions of story trees work best at first. Start with a simple story tree and don't overload it with ideas. As the discussion continues, you could ask the children to think about originality, plausibility and consistency within the story, and challenge any 'off the top of the head' ideas. Once the children become more familiar with the game, encourage them to work independently.

More ideas

You could place smart stars on a story tree template before the children begin, to encourage creative thinking. Story trees are essentially visual resources, so the larger the template, the better. Wall display trees are highly effective. The children could use story trees to retell stories they have read. They can change individual incidents and show on the tree how this might affect the story's plot.

Linked activities

Story trees can be successfully combined with **Character thumbnails**, **Setting thumbnails**, **Smart stars** and **Story motifs**.

Mystery hotel

A story that starts simply can go in all kinds of directions.

- Plan what happens next on this story tree. Start at the bottom and read along the branches.

- Fill in the empty leaves with your own ideas.

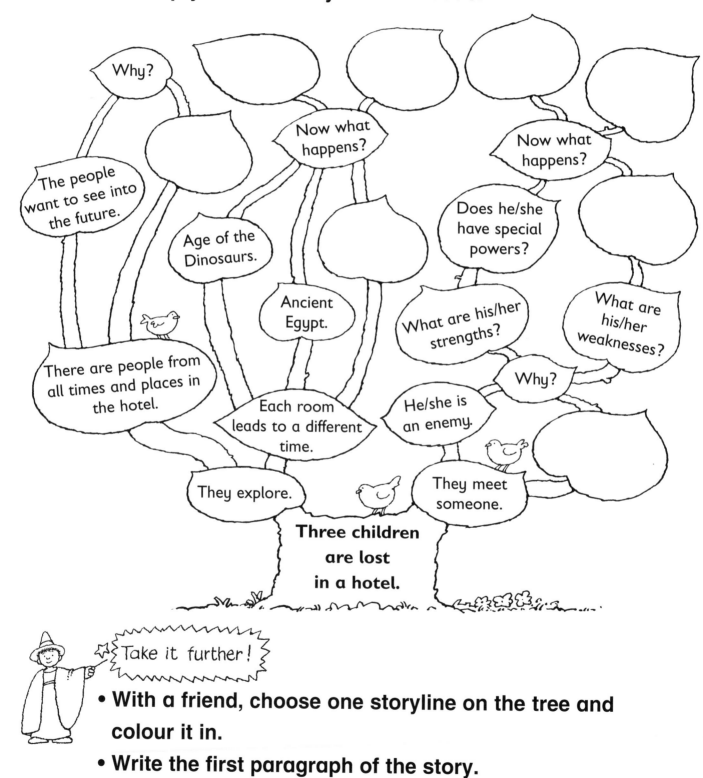

Why?

Now what happens?

Now what happens?

The people want to see into the future.

Does he/she have special powers?

Age of the Dinosaurs.

Ancient Egypt.

What are his/her strengths?

What are his/her weaknesses?

There are people from all times and places in the hotel.

Why?

Each room leads to a different time.

He/she is an enemy.

They explore.

They meet someone.

Three children are lost in a hotel.

☆ Take it further!

- **With a friend, choose one storyline on the tree and colour it in.**

- **Write the first paragraph of the story.**

Teachers' note The children could imagine the effect of moving characters from one period in history to another as they travel along the story tree. Ask them to think about how the story might be different if it were set in a different period.

What's the Story?
© A & C Black 2001

The magic box

- **Read the idea at the bottom of the story tree.**
- **Fill in the leaves with ideas for what happens next.**

A stranger sees them open the box.

Jade and Adam find a mysterious box.

Take it further!

- **Follow one of the storylines on the tree and colour it in.**
- **Write a description of each character.**

Teachers' note The text on this page can be masked before photocopying to provide a blank story tree on which the children can record story ideas.

What's the Story?
© A & C Black 2001

Contests

Taking a sentence out of context and suggesting possible meanings for it is good way to develop characters, settings and plots for a story. Even the simplest sentence can be interpreted in many different ways.

The games

The following activities aim to rouse the children's curiosity about a sentence by encouraging them to ask questions to discover its context and meaning. **Questions, questions!** introduces the children to the idea. **Spidergram** and **The secret of the door** provide practice in different ways of recording information and help children to think about the progression of a story. They will realise that the given sentence does not necessarily come at the start of the story, and that a discussion may need to 'explore backwards' to the beginning.

> **NLS:** Y3 T1 9,11 • Y4 T1 10 • Y4 T3 12,13 • Y5 T1 14,15 • Y6 T1 7

Tips

Before beginning the games, you could practise with the whole class by giving them a sentence out of context and asking them to think of questions that will help to give the sentence meaning. Make use of the 'big question words': where, when, what, why, who and how. The children can then answer the questions; encourage them to keep their responses brief, simple and focused, to avoid them drifting off into an 'and then... and then...' scenario. With the whole class, summarise and review the children's ideas, noting down the main points.

More ideas

Ask each child to choose a sentence from a book they have read and to write it in the centre of a spidergram. They could give the spidergram to another child, who has not read the book, to complete. The children can evaluate the resulting story possibilities and compare them with the storyline of the original book.

Linked activities

Profiles, Character thumbnails and **Setting thumbnails** can be used to make up background details for a sentence taken out of context.

Questions, questions!

These sentences come from different stories. If you haven't read the stories, it is difficult to understand the sentences.

- **For each sentence, think of a question you could ask to help you understand it.**

1. Only he understood the secret of the door.

   Where is the door?

2. They caught just a glimpse before it disappeared from sight.

   _____

3. This was the most precious thing she had ever owned, and now it might be gone forever.

   _____

4. And so they decided, and shook hands – although only Chris was smiling.

   _____

5. 'There were three things I told you to avoid,' he said. 'And now you have come across the worst of them!'

   _____

6. Smith lay slumped in the chair.

   _____

7. 'But I told you,' she protested, 'picking that colour could be dangerous!'

   _____

8. It was only when they thought the storm was over that the real trouble began.

   _____

9. Of all the days for this to happen, it had to be Friday.

   _____

10. Now that he had made the choice, life would never be quite the same again.

    _____

- **Discuss other questions you could ask.**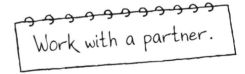

  Work with a partner.

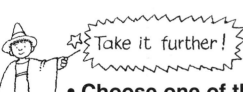
Take it further!

- **Choose one of the sentences and imagine the scene.**
- **Draw a picture of the scene. Write a caption to explain what is happening.**

Teachers' note The children could choose one of the sentences and use it to create a story map (see page 34). They could also link the sentences with story motifs they have created or with characters from character grids.

What's the Story?
© A & C Black 2001

Spidergram

- **Look at this spidergram. Read the sentence in the middle.**
- **Around the sentence are some questions you could ask about it.**
- **Think of some more questions and add them to the spidergram.**

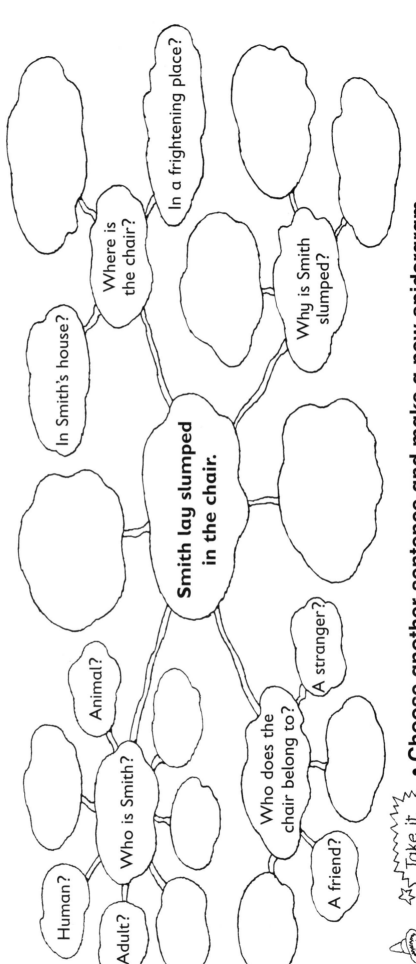

In a frightening place?

Where is the chair?

In Smith's house?

Why is Smith slumped?

Smith lay slumped in the chair.

Animal?

Who is Smith?

A stranger?

Who does the chair belong to?

Human?

Adult?

A friend?

Take it further!

- **Choose another sentence and make a new spidergram.**
- **Use a coin or a dice to answer the questions.**

Teachers' note For the extension activity, provide the children with the list of sentences on page 49. Alternatively, you could ask them to find a sentence themselves by looking in a story book.

What's the Story?
© A & C Black 2001

The secret of the door

- Read the sentence at the top of the story tree.
- Think about how the story might have got here. Work backwards to the story's beginning and write it on the tree trunk.
- Now work forwards along the other branches, thinking of other things that might happen.

You don't have to write in all the leaves.

- Only she knew the secret of the door.
- She stepped through the door, back to safety.
- The door was burned to ashes.

Take it further!

- Choose a sentence from a story you have read.
- Write it on a branch of a story tree.
- Fill in the tree to make new story ideas.

Teachers' note For the extension activity, the children could draw their own story trees or you could give them copies of this page with the text masked out. As a further game idea, they could write sentences at several points on a tree, and pass it to a partner to complete.

What's the Story?
© A & C Black 2001

Story masks

A story mask is part of a picture. It shows a tantalising portion of the whole scene — the visual equivalent of a context sentence — and is a useful way of concentrating on an individual incident in a story. It gives a writer the chance to consider how the story might have arrived at this point, and to think about what might happen next.

The games

In these games, the children are shown part of an illustration and encouraged to ask questions to find out what is happening. This is helpful for generating plot ideas and thinking creatively. It also develops the children's questioning and discussion skills. **What's going on?** and **Picture it** show a small portion of a picture, so that the children can imagine what else is going on out of view and what other characters might be in the whole picture. **A narrow escape** provides a fuller view of a scene and invites children to put their own interpretation on it.

NLS: Y3 T3 11 • Y4 T1 1 • Y4 T2 2 • Y5 T1 15

Tips

Before beginning the games, you could introduce story masks as a whole-class activity. Choose a picture and mask out all but a small portion. Ask the children to talk or write about what they think is happening, what has happened beforehand and what might happen next. Where possible, they should support their answers with evidence from the picture. Then reveal more of the picture and allow the children to revise or develop their ideas, until the whole picture is revealed. Emphasise that it doesn't matter if their impressions of the masked picture do not match what is happening in the whole picture.

More ideas

You can adapt these activities for use with any picture. Magazines and newspapers are good sources. When photocopying, it is helpful to use large sheets and allow a generous border, so that the children can write their ideas next to the picture. You could present a masked picture on an OHP for a whole-class discussion.

Linked activities

Use story masks with **Character thumbnails**, **Setting thumbnails** or **Story motifs** to suggest possible storylines. They can also be used with **Story trees**, by placing a picture at the start of the tree or on a branch.

What's going on?

- **This is part of a picture from a story.**
- **Make up some questions that could help you find out what is happening.**
- **Write them in the speech bubbles.**

Use these words: where, when, who, how, what, why.

How is the woman feeling?

☆ Take it further!

- **Write lists of possible answers to your questions.**
- **Decide the answers using a coin, a dice or your own ideas.**

What's the Story?
© A & C Black 2001

Picture it

- **This is part of a picture from a story.**
- **Make up some questions that could help you find out what is happening.**
- **Write them in the speech bubbles.**

Use these words: where, when, who, how, what, why.

- **Imagine the whole scene. Explain what you think is happening.**

_____

_____

_____

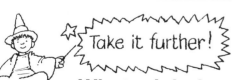

Take it further!

- **What might happen next?**
- **Continue the story.**

Teachers' note Encourage the children to think about different ways of interpreting the picture, for example, is the boy running away from an attacker, or has he stolen something?

What's the Story?
© A & C Black 2001

A narrow escape

This is a page from a novel called Roy Kane – TV Detective.
The girl in the picture is Roy's assistant, Vicki.

- Notice the different points of view used for the illustrations.
- Write in the box what you think is happening.
- Write in the speech bubbles.

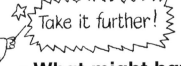

- **What might have happened just before this scene?**
- **What might happen next?**

Teachers' note The children could make character thumbnails for Vicki and Roy and use a coin or a dice to determine extra details. They could also write stories made up almost entirely of dialogue, based on these pictures.

What's the Story?
© A & C Black 2001

Exploring pictures

Exploring pictures is a good way of focusing on a story's mood, and helps a writer to understand how a sense of atmosphere can be created. A picture can also prompt ideas about plot, setting and characters through speculation about what might have happened and what is going to happen next.

The games

These activities present the children with a picture and a series of questions to help them think about the atmosphere the picture conjures up. The children are encouraged to use their skills of observation, deduction and speculation. It is best to begin with observation, as this allows children to 'start safe'. The games give children the opportunity to generate lots of ideas about atmosphere and will help them to produce similar ideas even when there is no picture, enabling them to imagine a scene much more vividly.

> **NLS:** Y3 T1 1 • Y3 T2 2 • Y3 T3 5,12 • Y4 T1 1 • Y4 T2 2 • Y5 T2 13

Tips

Before beginning the activities, familiarise the children with stories in which atmosphere and mood are important features. Show the children how a story can build up feelings in the reader, such as suspense, fear and humour. These feelings suggest what kind of thing might happen next and make the reader want to find out what will happen.

More ideas

Artists often try to create a particular atmosphere in their work to provoke a certain reaction. Encourage children to think about what the artist in each case is trying to communicate and to use interesting vocabulary that matches the atmosphere. You could make lists of atmospheric words they can draw on when writing their own stories.

Linked activities

These games can be used with many of the other ideas in the book, such as **Character thumbnails**, **Setting thumbnails** and **Story motifs**. Focusing on atmosphere can be done very effectively through the use of **Story notebooks**.

The rope swing

You can make up a story by 'jumping into' a picture and pretending you are there at the scene. It might be a real picture or a picture in your imagination.

• **Look at the picture and describe what you see.**

• **Answer the questions.**

> Work with a friend.

1. If this picture were in colour, what colours would you see?

_____

_____

2. Imagine there are sounds in the picture. What sounds can you hear?

_____

_____

3. What words describe the expressions on the children's faces?

_____

_____

• **Write some more questions about the picture.**

_____   _____

_____   _____

_____   _____

☆ Take it further!

Imagine you and your friend are the characters in the picture.

• **Describe how each of you is feeling.**

• **Make up some dialogue. Decide how the scene might end.**

Teachers' note This picture is by illustrator Jamie Egerton. The activities can also be carried out using reproduction of paintings. Those by Pieter Brueghel the Elder, L S Lowry, Stanley Spencer and Paulo Uccello are ideal.

What's the Story?
© A & C Black 2001

The dragon flies by

- **Look at the picture and describe what you see.**
- **Answer the questions on a separate piece of paper.**

Work with a friend.

1. How do you think the man is feeling?

2. What expression would be on his face?

3. If you were standing next to the man, how would you feel?

4. If the man told you about the dragon later, how would you react?

5. Think of other situations that could cause the feelings the man is having.

Take it further!

- **Imagine you are the man in the picture. Describe what happens next.**

Teachers' note The pictures on pages 58–60 are by illustrator Stella Hender. The children could work in groups, enacting the scene, developing it into a story and producing playscripts.

What's the Story?
© A & C Black 2001

A journey in the dark

- **Look at the picture and describe what you see.**
- **Answer the questions on a separate piece of paper.**

Work with a friend.

1. The picture is slightly tilted and the hedges are arching over the car. How does the artist want to make you feel?
2. Imagine there are two people in the car. Why are they making the journey?
3. Where do you think they are going?
4. What are they thinking?

Take it further!

- **Think of things that could happen next that would make the people** | excited |, | happy |, | nervous |, | terrified |, | curious | **or** | amused |.

Teachers' note The children could develop their story as a narrative poem. They first need to read examples of narrative poems about journeys.

What's the Story?
© A & C Black 2001

The hut in the woods

- **Look at the picture and describe what you see.**
- **Answer the questions on a separate piece of paper.**

Work with a friend.

1. How does the artist want to make you feel?

2. What or who might be inside the hut?

3. Make up two characters and imagine them in the picture. They feel very differently about why they are there. Describe their emotions.

4. What happens next?

Take it further!

- **Imagine you are describing the scene to someone who hasn't seen it. Write a paragraph about it.**

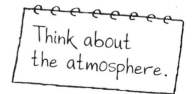

Think about the atmosphere.

Teachers' note This could be developed as a short story for a television advertisement. Make recordings of some 'story' advertisements and discuss some of the techniques and dialogue used. The children could write a storyline and stage or set directions based on the setting.

What's the Story?
© A & C Black 2001

Story notebooks

Storymaking happens in three stages – thinking, writing and editing. Drafting takes place through all three stages. In a story notebook, a writer can plan a story, record further ideas while writing without interrupting the flow, and note down observations and ideas while reviewing.

The game

The **Sample notebook** shows how notes can be made by both the child and teacher. It can be used as a teachers' reference, but could also be photocopied and shown to the children. **Using a notebook** introduces children to the format of a story notebook. This format should always be consistent – the children should write their story on the right-hand page and leave the left-hand page blank. This can then be used as follows:

- For the child and teacher to write reminders, notes and comments.
- For jotting down ideas and making notes before, during and after story-writing.
- For affixing 'prompts', such as pieces of clip art, thumbnails, motif cards, etc.
- For drawing mini story trees and spidergrams.
- For listing useful vocabulary.
- For the children to record their own assessment of the story.

> **NLS:** Y4 T2 14 • Y5 T2 13 • Y6 T1 7 • Y6 T3 7

Tips

Redrafting does not mean writing the story out again without making a mistake! An effective redraft is one where less useful ideas are taken out and more useful ideas are added; the balance and pace of the story are checked and altered if necessary; the vocabulary is reviewed, and the technical aspects of the work (punctuation, spelling and sentence structure) are tidied up. There is no golden rule about the number of redrafts but one or two should be enough.

More ideas

Briefly show the children ways in which they can annotate and edit their work, for example, by using standard editing marks such as:

insert ∧   delete ♂   make letter upper case ≡   make letter lower case ≢

Linked activities

Story trees and **Smart stars** can be used with a story notebook to provide ideas for improving the story.

Sample notebook

Anika has written her story on the right-hand page and recorded her thinking and checking on the left-hand page. There was also space on that page for the teacher to mention ideas for making her work even better.

Joanna Bradley is an extremely beautiful, popular, trendy girl who always manages to get into adventures. However, she always eventually escapes. Joanna has lovely soft, long golden hair cut in layers. She has an American accent, which sometimes sounds odd to the English people. She regularly wears a long black coat over a lilac strap-top (her favourite), set off with a silk scarf. Joanna is usually happy and excited to be alive – as though things had never been better.

One day Joanna set off with her family to see what was promised to be a fabulous firework show. At first the street where the bonfire party was held was dark, but as soon as the fireworks appeared the sky shone like a rainbow. The streaks and swirls of colour were all different; red, gold, silver blue – while the sounds were clamorous and ear-piercing. Joanna gasped delightedly as one huge rocket exploded into her favourite colour – bronze....

Anika Shah, Eastbury Farm School

Remember – sight, sound, smell, touch, feelings!
Oops – used 'always' twice!

Are you going to use this idea of her accent sounding odd later in the story? Steve
Yes, turn over two pages.
Avoid brackets.

I notice you change from present to past tense – did you intend this? Steve
No, I'll change it later.

I really like 'streaks and swirls'. Steve
Thanks (I just noticed I spelt 'rocket' wrong!)

Using a notebook

Use the left-hand page for your thinking and checking.

Title Important!

Opening sentence Make it vivid and strong.

First paragraph Short. Make the reader want to know more.

Dialogue Use early on to pep up the pace.

Write your story on the right-hand page.

Take it further!

• Once you have written the story, read it and decide if you want to change anything. Ask someone else to read it. What does he or she think?

What's the Story?
© A & C Black 2001

Suggestions for further reading

The following list provides suggestions of books and resources for encouraging creative thinking.

All Our Futures: Creativity, Culture and Education (Report to the DfEE from the National Advisory Committee on Creative and Cultural Education, 1999)

Biddulph, S. *The Secret Of Happy Children,* Thorsons, 1993

Bowkett, S. *Imagine That (a handbook of creative learning activities for the classroom),* Network Educational Press, 1997
Self-Intelligence (a handbook for developing confidence, self-esteem and interpersonal skills), Network Educational Press, 1999

Claxton, G. *Hare Brain Tortoise Mind,* Fourth Estate, 1998

De Bono, E. *Teach Your Child How To Think,* Pelican, 1993

Dilts, R. and Epstein, T. *Dynamic Learning,* Meta Publications, 1995

von Franz, M-L. *Shadow And Evil In Fairy Tales,* Shambala, 1995

Gawain, S. *Creative Visualisation,* Bantam Books, 1982

Goldberg, P. *The Intuitive Edge,* Turnstone Press, 1985

Goleman, D. *Emotional Intelligence,* Bloomsbury, 1996

Goleman, D., Kaufman, P. and Ray, M. *The Creative Spirit,* Dutton, 1992

Hall, C. and E., Leech, A. *Scripted Fantasy In The Classroom,* Routledge, 1990

Hickman, D.E. and Jacobson, S. *The Power Process: an NLP approach to writing,* Anglo-American Book Company, 1997

LeBoeuf, M. *Creative Thinking,* Piatkus, 1994

O'Connor, J. and Seymour, J. *Introducing Neuro-Linguistic Programming,* Mandala, 1990

Schnieder, M. and Killick, J. *Writing For Self Discovery,* Element, 1998

Smith, A. *Accelerated Learning In Practice,* Network Educational Press, 1998

Von Oech, R. *A Whack On The Side Of The Head: how you can be more creative,* Thorsons, 1990

Zipes, J. *Creative Storytelling,* Routledge, 1995

First published in 2001 by A & C Black (Publishers) Ltd
37 Soho Square, London W1D 3QZ

ISBN 0-7136-5420-1

A CIP catalogue record for this book is available from the British Library.

Printed by Caligraving Ltd, Thetford, Norfolk